REX

Collections

The Beatles
on Television

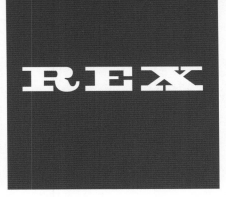

Collections

The Beatles
on Television

Jeff Bench
Ray Tedman

Reynolds & Hearn Ltd
London

The authors would like to express their gratitude for the help
received from the following people during the preparation of this book:
Robert Bailey, Chris Bentley, Mick Capewell, the late Mark Davis,
Kasper De Graaf, Martin Gainsford, Sandy Ganung, Marcus Hearn,
Jim McAlwane, The Magical Mystery Tour (Liverpool), Glen Marks,
The National Trust Team at Mendips, David Pratt, Ian Rakoff,
David Redfern, Carolynn Reynolds, Richard Reynolds, Ty Silkman,
Jim Yoakum, and all at Rex Features

Special thanks to Geoff Emerick, May Pang and Bob Whitaker,
for sharing their insights

RIP Mark, spirit of the age

First published in 2008
This edition first published in 2009 by
Reynolds & Hearn Ltd
61a Priory Road
Kew Gardens
Richmond
Surrey TW9 3DH

A CIP catalogue for this book is available from the British Library.

ISBN 978-1-905287-88-8

Designed by Chris Bentley
Printed and bound in Malta by Progress Press Co. Ltd.

Contents

'Do you like being famous?'
'Well, it's not like in your day, you know.'
An apparently adlibbed exchange between Eric Morecambe and John Lennon,
The Morecambe and Wise Show, 18 April 1964 (recorded 2 December 1963)

'Keep going, Bongo!' – Eric Morecambe, to Ringo Starr, from the same show

Thank Your Lucky Stars, 14 November 1964

Preface:
Not Like in Your Day

Like almost everything else they were involved in, the Beatles changed the medium of television.

This was not something they set out to accomplish. It happened as a result of the collision between their way of doing things, and the way that television did things, back in that strange, antediluvian, black-and-white world usually known as the Early Sixties. The Early Sixties were a continuation of the Fifties, only less exciting and more globally dangerous. The icons of the previous era were running out of steam. Elvis Presley was back from the Army but not playing Rock 'n' Roll. Marilyn Monroe had died in August 1962. John F Kennedy, the spirit of the age, had brought the world back from the brink of nuclear war during the Cuba Missile Crisis in October 1962, only to be gunned down the following year. In Germany, in August 1961, the Berlin Wall began to go up. In Britain, the ruling Conservative Party was to be undermined by the scandalous sex-and-spies Profumo Affair in 1963 – a thorough routing of the old guard in which the power of television was to play a key role. No one can say for sure when the Early Sixties ended, but one date has a very strong claim: 9 February 1964, the day the Beatles first appeared on American television on *The Ed Sullivan Show*. Already worshipped by fans in Britain and many other parts of Europe, the Beatles' conquest of America – through the medium of television – redrew the map of pop music and established the Fab Four as global superstars. Nothing was ever the same again. The real Sixties had begun.

It is difficult to express just how different television was before the great loosening of culture that took place from 1963-64 onwards. In Britain, where television today constantly strives to be accessible and 'relevant', it is hard to picture an era when television made no attempt to reflect ordinary manners or popular culture, but was used as a vehicle for imposing from above a particular set of values. Perhaps a single image can best sum up the nature of that remote era: in the 1950s, BBC television newscasters were required to read the evening news wearing dinner jackets.

The BBC's rival Independent Television ('Commercial Television', as it was called by some – to emphasize the importance of advertising revenue) began broadcasting in Britain in 1956. The Parliamentary Bill to licence the Independent Television Corporation had been bitterly opposed by the Labour Party (who promised to abolish ITV once elected to government, a promise – or threat – which they quietly forgot once in power). It was also opposed by many of all political persuasions in the House of Lords, Britain's Upper House. Prominent opponents of Commercial Television included the philosopher Bertrand Russell and novelist EM Forster. The language used in the debate frequently bordered on the apocalyptic. Lord Esher warned of a 'planned and premeditated orgy of vulgarity', while the Earl of Listowel predicted 'the lowest common denominator of taste' and 'crude and trivial entertainment'. Former Labour Foreign Secretary Herbert Morrison warned of the dangers to 'the future thinking of our people and our standards of culture', while Lord Hailsham compared the prospect of Independent Television to the Israelites' worship of the Golden Calf.

The Bill, nevertheless, was duly passed, in spite of such apoplectic ranting. Strangely, British civilisation and culture did not crumble and vanish overnight. But a certain whiff of social change did seem to be in the air in the later Fifties, a foreshadowing of the social revolution of the forthcoming decade. Whether it was the Angry Young Men of the theatre and literature, the cosmopolitan raciness of the James Bond novels, the explicit power of the movies emerging from Hammer Films, the new 'continental' coffee bar culture, or the first timid emergence of indigenous British rock 'n' roll, there was a new spirit abroad. But this questioning and non-deferential attitude was not yet part of the British cultural mainstream. It had to be sought out. In the 1960s, the Beatles – and others – brought this new classless, democratic zeitgeist into every home in the land. Welcome or unwelcome, as the case might be.

What a difference a few years can make. In September 1969, in the run up to the release of *Abbey Road*, an entire edition of BBC2's leading arts programme *Late Night Line-Up* was devoted to a preview and analysis of the new Beatles album. In 1963, the idea that a 'serious' arts programme would pay any attention at all to a pop group would have been unthinkable. This book tells the story – in words, but mainly through photographs – of how the Beatles participated in and benefitted from that sea-change in broadcasting. Tracing the Beatles' TV career resembles taking an instant crash course in media studies – except that the Beatles (nearly) always make it fun.

Rex Collections: The Beatles on Television is primarily concerned with the Beatles as performers on TV. The humour and irreverence of the Beatles during their many television interviews could be the subject of a book in itself – and probably will be, some day.

Jeff Bench and Ray Tedman
March 2008

Performing 'I Want To Hold Your Hand'
on Granada's *Late Scene Extra*, 25 November 1963

McCartney, Harrison and Lennon
filmed at The Carvern Club, Liverpool,
22 August 1962

1962:
From The Cavern to Granadaland

On 22 August 1962 the Organisation armée secrète (OAS), a group made up largely of French settlers in Algeria and their sympathisers, attempted to assassinate the French president Charles de Gaulle, raking his Citroen DS with machine gun fire. The same day a crew from the Granada Television programme *Know the North* were filming a lunchtime performance by the Beatles in the Cavern Club in Liverpool – the first and only professionally made film with synchronised sound of a performance by the group in its definitive line-up of John, Paul, George and Ringo on the stage of the club they made internationally famous.

There are several versions of the film. Because of doubts about the quality of the filming it did not appear on *Know the North* and was not broadcast until 6 November 1963 on *Scene at 6.30*, by which time the fame of the group outweighed quality considerations. The version transmitted was shot from the back of the Cavern with a single camera and featured the Beatles singing the Lieber/Stoller/Barrett song 'Some Other Guy'. A second version of this sequence with a cutaway inserted showing the Beatles from the back of the stage was created in the 1970s when the original film was damaged. A third version can be seen in *The Beatles Anthology*. The film features two minutes of a performance of 'Some Other Guy' with cutaways to show audience reaction. There are also cutaways of the band taken from performances of several other songs. The performance of 'Some Other Guy' is a completely different version, filmed at the Cavern on the same day, synched with the audio of the original version.

Granada Television had, probably unknowingly, captured the group at a pivotal moment. On 4 June the Beatles had signed with EMI and on 6 June the group had recorded four songs at EMI's Abbey Road Studios and had met George Martin for the first time. On the original version of the film there is a cry from the audience of 'We want Pete!' Pete Best, the band's drummer for two years, had been sacked on 16 August to be replaced by Ringo Starr. On the day after filming John married his long-time girlfriend Cynthia Powell.

On 11 September 1962 the Beatles recorded the tracks for what was to be their first single at Abbey Road and on 5 October EMI released the disc, with 'Love Me Do' as the A-side and 'PS I Love You' as the B-side. Following the release of the record the group made their real first appearance on television with a live performance of 'Some Other Guy' and 'Love Me Do' on the Granada Television local news programme *People and Places*, transmitted on Wednesday 17 October 1962. They recorded a further performance on 29 October (transmitted on *People and Places* 2 November) playing 'Love Me Do' and 'A Taste of Honey'.

The Beatles were in London on 4 December for their first television appearance in the capital, appearing live on Associated-Rediffusion's children's programme *Tuesday Rendezvous*, miming the whole of 'Love Me Do' and the opening of 'PS I Love You'. Their final television appearance of 1962 was a live performance on *People and Places* transmitted on 17 December when the group performed 'Love Me Do' and 'PS I Love You'.

Val Parnell's Sunday Night at the London Palladium, 13 October 1963

1963:
Beatlemania

The word 'Beatlemania', coined in 1963, was emblematic of a year of frantic activity by the group – and a year of increasingly frantic coverage by the press, radio and television. With manager Brian Epstein in the driving seat, the Beatles embarked on a relentless series of one-night live performances, television and radio appearances and recording sessions. There were 28 television appearances, the most of any year of the group's existence. No physical record remains of the majority of these performances, and indeed of performances in later years.

On 11 January the group's second single 'Please Please Me' was released and on Sunday 13 January the Beatles were in a Birmingham television studio recording a mimed performance of what was to be their first UK number one for the ITV networked pop show *Thank Your Lucky Stars*. With a large teenage audience the show featured mimed performances of new record releases. This was a key moment for the Beatles – when the show was broadcast countrywide on 19 January it was the first time most people had seen the Beatles. (This wasn't the first television performance of 'Please Please Me', the group had mimed a performance on *Roundup*, a Scottish children's television programme broadcast live on 6 January.)

The Beatles were back in Manchester on 16 January for an appearance on *People and Places*, miming 'Please Please Me' and 'Ask Me Why'. On 17 February they were in the Teddington Studio Centre, south west of London, recording a new mimed version of 'Please Please Me' for the edition of *Thank Your Lucky Stars* broadcast on 23 February. Between television appearances the group were performing in such varied venues as the Assembly Hall in the Welsh town of Mold on Thursday 24 January and the Co-operative Hall in Darwen, Lancashire on 25 January (a performance promoted by the Baptist Youth Club promising non-stop dancing and a buffet – and all for six shillings). In February the Beatles started their first nationwide tour which was headlined by 16-year-old singing sensation Helen Shapiro (voted best British female singer in 1961 and 1962).

'Please Please Me' took the UK singles number one spot on 2 March. The same day the Beatles, together with Brian Epstein, appeared live for their first television interview on ABC Television's *ABC at Large*. Broadcast in the Midlands and north regions, the interview with David Hamilton included a clip of their 17 February performance of 'Please Please Me'.

Tuesday 9 April, the day after the birth of John's son Julian, saw the group miming live on Rediffusion's *Tuesday Rendezvous* ('From Me To You', 'Please Please Me'), a warm-up for their first BBC appearance on *The 625 Show*, which advertised itself as a showcase for 'up and coming young talent'. The programme was recorded at the BBC's London Lime Grove Studios on Saturday 13 March and was transmitted nationwide on 16 April, the Beatles performing 'From Me To You', 'Thank you Girl' and 'Please Please Me'. Following the BBC recording the group were in ABC's Teddington Studios, filming another appearance on *Thank Your Lucky Stars*, miming 'From Me To You', transmitted on 20 April.

On 22 March the group's first album *Please Please Me* was released, and on 11 April their third single 'From Me To You' hit the record stores. By 2 May the single was at number one, followed by the album on 4 May. From mid-April to the end of August the Beatles made nine television appearances, mostly following the existing pattern of mimed performances of a couple of songs. On 16 April there was a live mimed performance on Granada's *Scene at 6.30* ('From Me To You'), on 12 May a recorded performance of 'From Me To You' and 'I Saw Her Standing There' for *Thank Your Lucky Stars*. Transmitted on 18 May, for the first time on television the Beatles were the headline act. A second live performance on BBC television followed, on a children's show *Pops and Lenny*, hosted by puppet Lenny the Lion and ventriloquist Terry Hall, transmitted on 16 May with performances of 'From Me To You', 'Please Please Me' and 'After You've Gone'. A Mersey Beat special of *Lucky Stars (Summer Spin)*, recorded 23 June and transmitted 29 June featured 'From Me to You', and 'I Saw Her Standing There'. The transmission clashed with John's appearance as a juror on the BBC's *Juke Box Jury*. Then it was back to Granada on 14 August to record two songs for two separate editions of *Scene at 6.30* – 'Twist and Shout', transmitted the same day and 'She Loves You', transmitted 19 August. *Lucky Stars (Summer Spin)* beckoned again with a recording of a mimed performance of 'She Loves You' and 'I'll Get You', recorded 18 August 1963, transmitted 24 August. On 22 August the Southern regional television station recorded the Beatles miming 'She Loves You' for their programme *Day by Day*, transmitted the same day.

The Beatles' next television appearance was very different. BBC documentary film maker Don Haworth had been commissioned to make a programme about the Mersey Beat phenomenon. After discussions with Brian Epstein and the Beatles, Haworth had secured their agreement to appear in the film, partly because they felt that they would be able to discuss their work in more depth than would be possible on a normal pop programme. The shooting schedule involved four days (28 to 30 August), including live performances (Twist and Shout', 'She Loves You', 'Love Me Do'), interviews and backstage shots, a

mock arrival at Speke Airport, a ferry trip across the Mersey and, on the fourth day, extended coverage of Ringo and George. The finished documentary, which included interviews and footage of other groups and fans of the Liverpool music scene, was first transmitted with a restricted regional coverage on 9 October 1963 with a national airing on 13 November. The programme was well received as an insightful piece of filmmaking – many clips from the documentary have resurfaced over the years in subsequent films about the Beatles.

The variety show had been a staple of British television for many years, and in the last four months of 1963 the Beatles were seen on four of the most popular. On 1 September the group appeared on Mike and Bernie Winters's *Big Night Out*, a popular ITV show hosted by the Winters brothers who had gained fame as a comedy double act. The group's appearance was a very straightforward affair with performances of 'From Me To You', 'She Loves You', 'I Saw Her Standing There' and 'Twist and Shout'. The programme, recorded in front of a studio audience, was transmitted on 7 September 1963.

After the rather staid variety show format the Beatles' next television outing was on Associated Rediffusion's *Ready, Steady, Go!*, a live music programme with an audience aimed squarely at a youth market. With its bare studio, in-shot cameras, informal style and slogan 'The Weekend Starts Here!', the programme, launched in August 1963, perfectly captured the spirit of the times. The group's first performance was on Friday 4 October 1963 when they mimed to 'Twist and Shout', 'I'll Get You', and 'She Loves You'. A feature of the show was a competition where four teenage girls mimed to Brenda Lee's 'Let's Jump the Broomstick', with the winner selected by Paul. In a curious twist, the winner, Melanie Coe, was to feature in the news story that inspired him to write 'She's Leaving Home' in 1967.

It's easy to overplay particular events in a group's history, and their rise and fall is the result of a complex set of factors. Notwithstanding this caveat, the Beatles' appearance on *Val Parnell's Sunday Night at the London Palladium* was one of their pivotal moments. Hosted by the genial Bruce Forsyth, the show was the market leader in

Val Parnell's Sunday Night at the London Palladium, 13 October 1963

Val Parnell's Sunday Night at the London Palladium, 13 October 1963

British television variety, and an appearance on the top of the bill was a major event. Broadcast live, 15 million viewers saw the group play 'From Me To You', 'I'll Get You', 'She Loves You', and 'Twist and Shout' in front of an ecstatic audience. Incredibly, no visual record of this performance exists, although there is an audio tape and a short piece of newsreel, including an interview with George, Paul and Ringo.

On 18 October it was back from national to local with a mimed performance of 'She Loves You' for Granada's *Scene at 6.30*, and then another session for *Thank Your Lucky Stars* covering 'All My Loving', 'Money (That's What I Want)' and 'She Loves You' on 20 October, transmitted on 26 October, three days after the Beatles had flown to Sweden for their first foreign tour.

The group were in Sweden from 23 to 31 October, and as well as their concert tour they recorded four songs for the Sveriges Television pop show *Drop In*. Recorded in front of an audience, the Beatles played (as planned) 'She Loves You' and 'Twist and Shout' and then, encouraged by the host and the enthusiasm of the audience, two encores, 'I Saw Her Standing There' and 'Long Tall Sally'. The session, recorded on 30 October, was broadcast on 3 November.

The following evening the Beatles were on stage in front of the British 'establishment', performing at the Royal Command Performance at London's Prince of Wales Theatre. The audience, led by the Queen Mother, Princess Margaret and her husband Lord Snowdon, heard the group play 'From Me To You', 'She Loves You', 'Till There Was You', and 'Twist and Shout'. In characteristically sardonic manner, introducing 'Twist and Shout', John announced 'For our last number I'd like to ask for your help. Would the people in the cheaper seats clap your hands, and the rest of you, if you just rattle your jewellery.' The whole show was recorded by Associated Television and broadcast on 10 November 1963. On 22 November the Beatles' new album *With the Beatles* was released, on 28 November 'She Loves You' returned to the number one spot in the UK single charts for two weeks and on 29 November the new single 'I Want To Hold Your Hand' was released.

There was still time for Granada Television. On 25 November the group were back in Manchester to record two tracks. They mimed to 'I Want To Hold Your Hand' and were interviewed with comedian Ken Dodd for *Late Scene Extra* (broadcast on 27 November) and then mimed to 'This Boy' for transmission on *Scene at 6.30* on 20 December.

The Beatles recorded their fourth and final variety show of the year on 2 December when they made an appearance on ATV's top-rated *The Morecambe and Wise Show*. The slightly anarchic style of the Eric Morcambe and Ernie Wise double act seemed to fit with the group's deadpan humorous style. As well as singing three numbers, 'This Boy', 'All My Loving' and 'I Wanna Hold Your Hand', the Beatles joined Eric and Ernie for a sketch, ending (after a change of costume to striped blazers and boaters) with a performance with Ernie of part of the song 'On Moonlight Bay'. The show was first broadcast on 18 April 1964. In retrospect, although the group seem to participate happily enough, there is something slightly uncomfortable about the performance, as if they are already beginning to outgrow the accepted style of mainstream entertainment.

As 1963 drew to a close, such was the work rate of the Beatles that there were three more performances for the television audience. On 7 December the group held a special concert for their Northern Area Fan Club in Liverpool. Filmed by the BBC, it was transmitted the same day as a thirty minute programme titled *It's the Beatles*, with performances of 'From Me To You', 'I Saw Her Standing There', 'All My Loving', 'Roll Over Beethoven', 'Boys', 'Till There Was You', 'She Loves You', 'This Boy', 'I Want To Hold Your Hand', 'Money (That's What I Want)', and 'Twist and Shout'. The same day the BBC recorded an all-Beatles *Juke Box Jury* which was transmitted before *It's the Beatles* to an audience of 23 million viewers.

Finally, on 15 December, the group recorded mimed performances of 'All My Loving', 'Twist and Shout', 'She Loves You', and 'I Want To Hold Your Hand' for a special Mersey sound edition of *Thank Your Lucky Stars* to be broadcast on 21 December. On 12 December 'I Want To Hold Your Hand' had reached number one in the UK singles chart, where it lodged for the next five weeks.

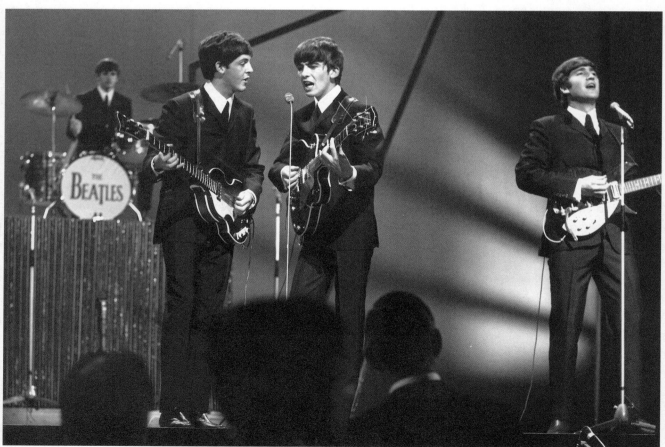

Above and opposite:
Backstage at the London Palladium,
13 October 1963

Thank Your Lucky Stars, 18 October 1963

Opposite: On stage and backstage for *Val Parnell's
Sunday Night at the London Palladium*, 13 October 1963

Above and opposite:
The Royal Command Performance,
Prince of Wales Theatre, London,
4 November 1963

Dressing Rooms 25-27
Wardrobe Dept

At ATV Studios, Borehamwood, for the recording of
The Morecambe and Wise Show, 2 December 1963

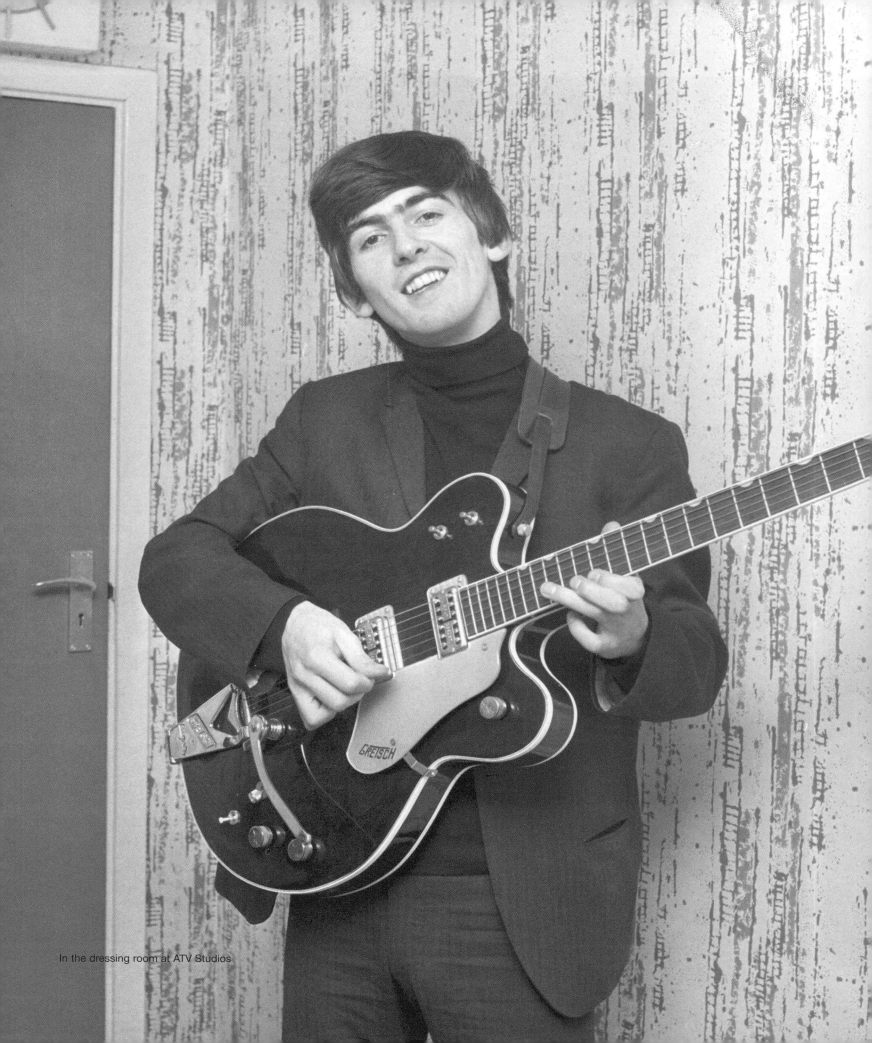

In the dressing room at ATV Studios

Recording *The Morecambe and Wise Show*, 2 December 1963

The Ed Sullivan Show, 9 February 1964, recording material that would be transmitted on the 23 February 1964 show

1964:
America ...
and Afterwards

This was the year that the Beatles hit America, but even before they landed for the first time at New York's John F Kennedy International Airport on 7 February, American television viewers had caught a glimpse of the group in performance. NBC's *The Jack Parr Show*, broadcast on 3 January, included film of the Beatles performing 'She Loves You' (extracted from the BBC documentary *The Mersey Sound*) and 'From Me To You' (footage of a show in Bournemouth filmed on 16mm in November 1963).

Before their US tour the Beatles were back on *Sunday Night at the London Palladium*, broadcast live by Associated-Rediffusion on 12 January. As well as performing five songs ('I Want To Hold Your Hand', 'This Boy', 'All My Loving', 'Money (That's What I Want)' and 'Twist and Shout') the group performed a comedy sketch with host Bruce Forsyth.

The February trip to the US had been planned for several months but one unplanned event made the tour even more potent. On 1 February 'I Want to Hold Your Hand' topped the US singles chart and sat there for seven weeks. On 8 February the Beatles were rehearsing in CBS Television Studio 50, New York, the home of one of America's most popular variety programmes, *The Ed Sullivan Show*. Sullivan, a former entertainment columnist, had become a kingmaker, with an appearance on his show being the next thing to a surefire guarantee of stardom. The live show enjoyed enormous ratings in the 1950s and 1960s, with families sitting around the television every Sunday evening to watch. Sullivan had featured Bill Haley and His Comets in August 1955, singing 'Rock Around the Clock',

the first performance of a rock 'n' roll song on US national television. Elvis Presley's first performance on the show in September 1956 took his career into the stratosphere.

Brian Epstein understood the power of Sullivan's show and had arranged for the group to appear on three consecutive Sundays in February. The first performance, broadcast on 9 February 1964, drew an audience of some 73 million. The Beatles played 'All My Loving', 'Till There Was You', 'She Loves You', 'I Saw Her Standing There' and 'I Want to Hold Your Hand' to a live studio audience composed largely of screaming teenage girls. The following week the Beatles were on the show again, broadcasting from Miami Beach, Florida. The set started with 'From Me to You', followed by 'This Boy', 'All My Loving', 'I Saw Her Standing There', concluding with 'I Want to Hold Your Hand'. Their final appearance was on 23 February, in a taped segment recorded earlier in the day on 9 February. They played three numbers, 'Twist and Shout', 'Please Please Me' and 'I Want to Hold Your Hand'.

As well as the Ed Sullivan appearances, CBS filmed the Beatles playing a concert at the Washington DC Coliseum on Tuesday 11 February. An edited version was shown in a closed-circuit telecast in cinemas US-wide on 14 and 15 March. Documentary filmmakers David and Albert Maysles were given exclusive access to the behind-the-scenes working of the US tour. Granada Television, who had financed the filming, showed some of the hastily assembled footage under the title *Yeah! Yeah! Yeah! The Beatles in New York* in a 40-minute slot on the evening of 12 February. The final version of the documentary, *The Beatles in America*, was broadcast by CBS Television on 13 November 1964.

The group returned to the UK on 22 February. The following day, jet lagged or not, the Beatles were at the Teddington Studio Centre to record their second appearance on Mike and Bernie Winters's *Big Night Out*. After rehearsals the programme was recorded in front of a live audience, the session not finishing until 10.30pm. The group mimed 'All My Loving, 'I Wanna Be Your Man', 'Till There Was You' and joined in a few sketches.

Taking a break from filming their first feature film *A Hard Day's Night*, the Beatles appeared live on *Ready, Steady, Go!* on 20 March, miming 'It Won't Be Long', 'Can't Buy Me Love', and 'You Can't Do That'. On 21 March 'She Loves You' took the number one spot in the US singles chart. On 23 March John Lennon's first book *In His Own Write* was published. On 2 April 'Can't Buy Me Love' topped the UK chart and on 4 April it was number one in the US chart. The group occupied the top five positions in the American chart and eleven other places in the top one hundred. The Beatles topped the bill at the *New Musical Express* Annual Poll Winner's Concert on 26 April, receiving an award from actor Roger Moore. They sang 'She Loves You', 'You Can't Do That', 'Twist and Shout', 'Long Tall Sally' and 'Can't Buy Me Love'. A recording of the show was transmitted by ABC Television on 10 May 1964.

After a day of rehearsals on 27 April the group recorded a TV special *Around the Beatles* at Wembley Studios in front of a studio audience. As well as singing an eleven song set ('Twist and Shout', 'Roll Over Beethoven', 'I Wanna Be Your Man', a medley of 'Love Me Do/Please Please Me/From Me to You/She Loves You/I Want to Hold Your Hand', 'Can't Buy Me Love', and 'Shout') the group appeared in a sketch which was a spoof of part of Shakespeare's *A Midsummer Night's Dream*. The 60-minute show was transmitted nationally by Rediffusion on 6 May 1964.

Thursday 4 June saw the Beatles (minus Ringo, who had tonsillitis) with stand-in drummer Jimmy Nicol depart for a 27-day five-country tour. On 5 June the group taped a show for the Dutch television company VARA-tv. In the first half of the show they fielded questions from the audience translated into English by one of the hosts, in the second they mimed to 'Twist and Shout', 'All My Loving', 'Roll Over Beethoven', 'Long Tall Sally', 'She Loves You' and 'Can't Buy Me Love'. Although they were miming the mikes were left open, and so it's possible to hear the live performance as well. The session was broadcast on television station Netherlands 1 on Monday 8 June.

By the time the Beatles got to Australia, Ringo was back with the band. On 17 June the last of six Melbourne concerts was taped in its entirety by Australian Channel 9.

Nine songs were selected and packaged into a *Beatles Sing for Shell* special (the Shell company being the sponsor of the programme). The set, transmitted on 1 July 1964, was 'I Saw Her Standing There', 'You Can't Do That', 'All My Loving', 'She Loves You', 'Till There Was You', 'Roll Over Beethoven', 'Can't Buy Me Love', 'This Boy' and 'Long Tall Sally'.

Back in the UK at the beginning of July, the Beatles were at the BBC's Lime Grove Studios on 7 July (Ringo's 24th birthday) to tape three songs for future editions of the BBC chart show *Top of the Pops*. They mimed 'A Hard Day's Night' and 'Long Tall Sally', transmitted on 8 July, and 'Things We Said Today', transmitted 29 July. On 11 July the group mimed live on ABC Television's *Lucky Stars (Summer Spin)*, covering 'A Hard Day's Night', 'Long Tall Sally', 'Things We Said Today' and 'You Can't Do That'.

In spite of their international fame the Beatles continued to appear on what, today, seem very cheesy variety shows – which perhaps says much more about the nature of British television at the time rather than any lack of judgement by the group and by Brian Epstein. On 19 July the Beatles appeared on Mike and Bernie Winters's live *Blackpool Night Out*, taking part in several sketches and singing 'A Hard Days Night', 'And I Love Her', 'If I Fell', 'Things We Said Today' and 'Long Tall Sally'. 'A Hard Day's Night' topped the chart in the UK on 23 July, followed by the US chart on 1 August.

Following an extensive North American tour in August, the next time the group was in a television studio was on 3 October, when they taped a live performance of three songs ('Kansas City/Hey Hey Hey Hey', 'I'm a Loser' and 'Boys') in front of an audience of Beatles Fan Club members for Jack Good's primetime American pop show *Shindig*. On 14 October they were back in Granada Television's studios in Manchester to record a mimed performance of 'I Should Have Known Better' for *Scene at 6.30*.

Three sessions in November finished the Beatles' television performance commitments for 1964. They were at Teddington Studios on 14 November, to tape a mimed set ('I Feel Fine', 'She's a Woman', 'I'm a Loser' and 'Rock and Roll Music') for an edition of *Thank Your Lucky Stars* to be broadcast on 21 November. On 16 November they were at Riverside Studios in Hammersmith miming 'I Feel Fine' and 'She's a Woman' for an edition of *Top of the Pops*, broadcast later that day. Finally, on 23 November, the Beatles made their swansong for *Ready, Steady, Go!*, miming 'I Feel Fine', 'She's a Woman', 'Baby's in Black' and 'Kansas City/Hey Hey Hey Hey'.

On 10 December 'I Feel Fine' was at number one in the UK and on 26 December it was number one in the US.

Val Parnell's Sunday Night at the London Palladium,
12 January 1964

Above and opposite:
Val Parnell's Sunday Night at the London Palladium,
12 January 1964

Crowds outside CBS-TV Studio 50, New York, in advance of the Beatles' first appearance on *The Ed Sullivan Show*, 9 February 1964

Opposite:
Big Night Out, 23 February 1964

Below: The Beatles' second appearance on *The Ed Sullivan Show*, 16 February 1964, a live broadcast from the Deaville Hotel, Miami Beach, Florida

Right:
Big Night Out,
23 February 1964

Below and opposite:
Ready, Steady, Go!,
20 March 1964

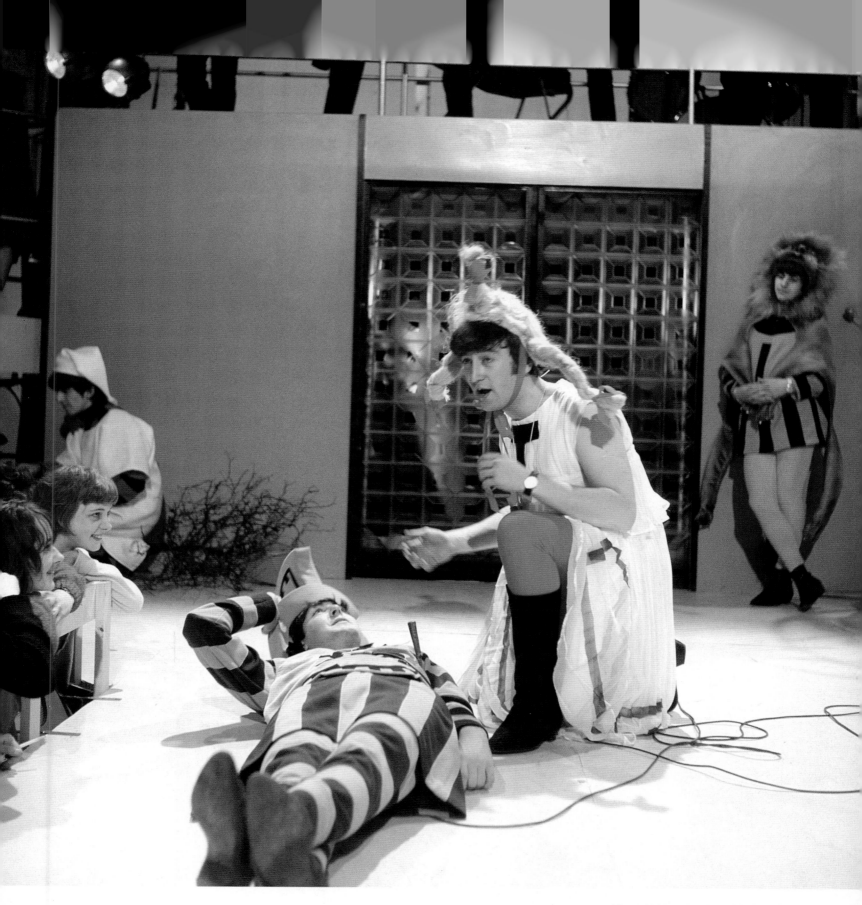

The *A Midsummer Night's Dream* sketch
on *Around the Beatles*, 28 April 1964

Opposite:
Around the Beatles, 28 April 1964

Around the Beatles, 28 April 1964

George, Paul, John and substitute drummer Jimmy Nicol interviewed for VARA-tv's *De Beatles in Nederland*, 5 June 1964

John, Paul, George and Jimmy perform at the
Café-Restaurant Treslong in Hillegom, Holland
for VARA-tv's *De Beatles in Nederland*,
5 June 1964

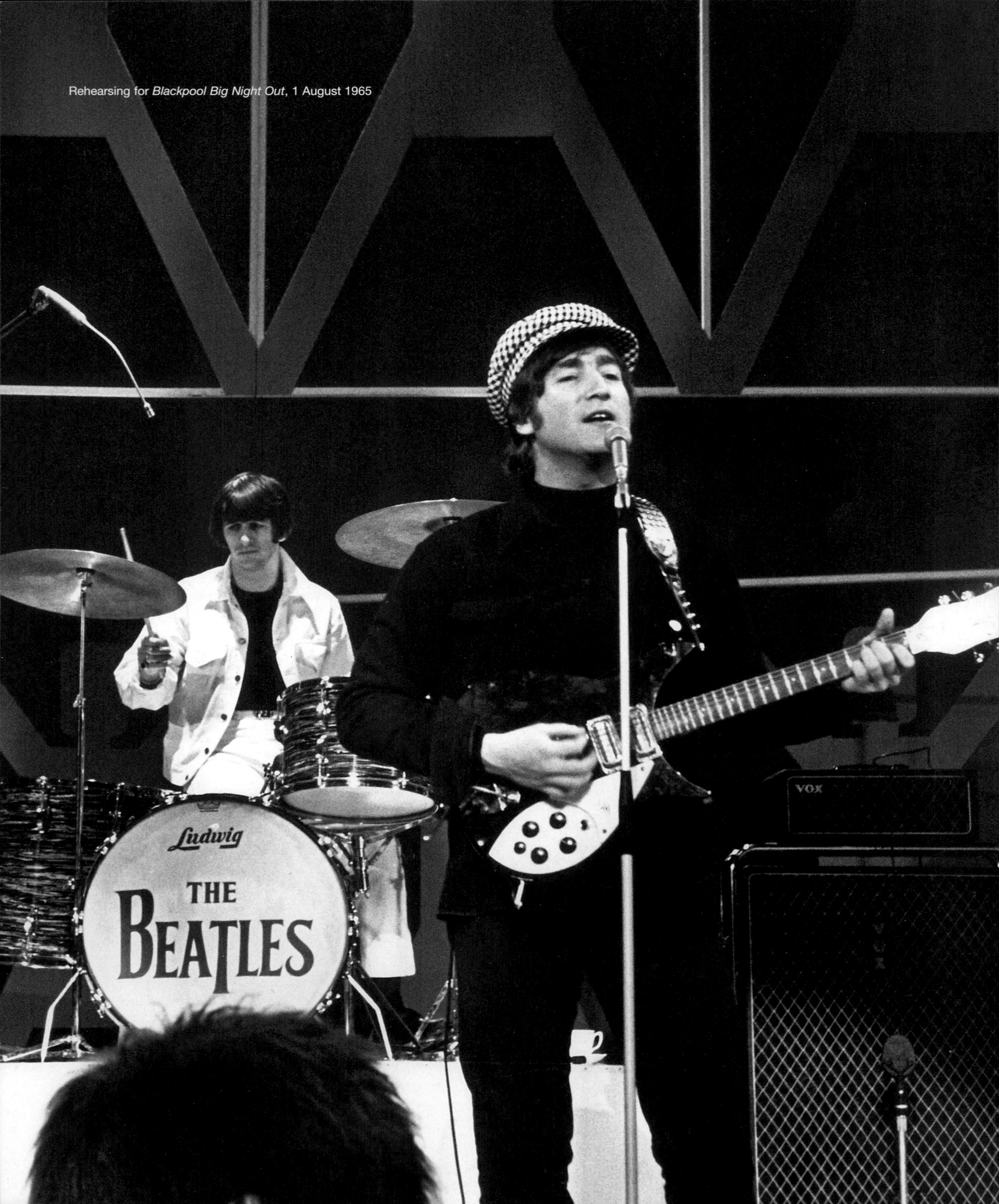

Rehearsing for *Blackpool Big Night Out*, 1 August 1965

1965-67:
Pleasing Themselves

1965 was a transitional year for the Beatles. Although it was superficially similar to 1964 – they made another film and they did a North American, European and UK tour – the difference was that John, Paul, George and Ringo decided to start pleasing themselves rather than everybody else. One of the results of this was that their television performances wound down.

On 28 March, during the filming of *Help!*, the group recorded their final performances for *Thank Your Lucky Stars* at Alpha Studios in Birmingham. They mimed to 'Eight Days a Week', 'Yes It Is', and 'Ticket to Ride' in front of a studio audience. The show was broadcast on 3 April 1965. 'Ticket to Ride' and 'Yes It Is' were again mimed at the BBC's Riverside Studios on 10 April for an edition of *Top of the Pops* broadcast on 15 April.

As in 1964, the Beatles performed live at the *New Musical Express* Annual Poll Winners All Star Concert at the Empire Pool, Wembley. On 11 April, in front of an audience of 10,000, they performed 'I Feel Fine', 'She's a Woman', 'Baby's in Black', 'Ticket to Ride' and 'Long Tall Sally'. The show, filmed by ABC Television, was broadcast on 18 April 1965. Also, later in the day on 11 April, the group appeared live on *The Eamonn Andrews Show*, miming 'Ticket to Ride' and 'Yes It Is'. On 13 April 'Eight Days a Week' topped the US chart, and on 2 April 'Ticket to Ride' was number one in the UK. To the pleasure of many and the censure of a few, the announcement that John, Paul, George and Ringo had been awarded MBEs was made in the Queen's Birthday Honours list on 12 June 1965.

On 20 June, the Beatles were in Paris kicking off a short European tour with two performances at the Palais des Sports. French television station Channel 2 recorded the complete set at the second performance ('Twist and Shout', 'She's a Woman', 'I'm a Loser', 'Can't Buy Me Love', 'Baby's in Black', 'I Wanna Be Your Man', 'A Hard Day's Night', 'Everybody's Trying to Be My Baby', 'Rock and Roll Music', 'I Feel Fine', 'Ticket to Ride', and 'Long Tall Sally'). The set (minus 'I Feel Fine') was broadcast on 31 October under the title *Les Beatles*. Returning from their European tour the Beatles made their fourth and final appearance with Mike and Bernie Winters on *Blackpool Night Out* to promote their new film *Help!* Transmitted live from the ABC Theatre on 1 August 1965, the group joined in banter with Mike and Bernie and performed 'I Feel Fine', 'I'm Down', 'Act Naturally', 'Ticket to Ride', 'Yesterday' (a solo by Paul), and 'Help!'.

The Beatles left for their 1965 US tour on 13 August. On 14 August there were back in Studio 50 in New York recording a segment for *The Ed Sullivan Show* in front of a live audience. They performed the same set, in the same order, which they had played on *Blackpool Night Out*. The show was broadcast on 13 September.

The following day the Beatles performed in New York's Shea Stadium in front of 55,600 fans, creating a new world record for audience size and revenue. The whole event, including the helicopter ride to the stadium, the journey in the Wells Fargo armoured truck to the stage, the concert and backstage events, was filmed by Ed Sullivan's Sullivan Productions. This footage became *The Beatles at Shea Stadium*, a 50-minute colour television special, which had its world premiere on BBC Television on 1 March 1966, and its US television premiere on 10 January 1967. The show doesn't include the full set, but includes the following numbers: 'Twist and Shout', 'I Feel Fine', 'Dizzy Miss Lizzy', 'Ticket to Ride', 'Act Naturally', 'Can't Buy Me Love', 'Baby's in Black', 'A Hard Day's Night', 'Help!' and 'I'm Down'. On 4 September 'Help!' was at number one in the US chart and on 26 of the month the Beatles received their MBEs from the Queen at Buckingham Palace. 'Yesterday' took the US top spot on 9 October, John's 25th birthday.

At the beginning of November the Beatles were back at Granada Television in Manchester, working on a TV special *The Music of Lennon and McCartney*. Rehearsed and recorded on 1 and 2 November, the programme featured a number of artists performing John and Paul's songs as well as the group miming 'Day Tripper' and 'We Can Work It Out'. Paul sang 'Yesterday' with Marianne Faithful. The show was first transmitted on 16 December 1965, the same day that 'We Can Work it Out/Day Tripper' was number one in the UK.

Later in November the Beatles took a path which meant that, in the future, most television performances would be promotional videos produced by the group. On 23 November they recorded videos for five songs: 'We Can Work It Out' (three versions), 'Day Tripper' (three versions), 'Help!', 'Ticket to Ride', and 'I Feel Fine' (two versions). More promos were shot on 19 and 20 May 1966: 'Paperback Writer' (four versions) and 'Rain' (three versions). The second day of shooting took place at Chiswick House in London, shot on 35mm colour stock.The director was Michael Lindsay-Hogg, who had worked on *Ready, Steady, Go!* On 16 June the Beatles appeared live on *Top of the Pops* and mimed to 'Paperback Writer' and 'Rain', the last time the group mimed on a pop television show. 'Paperback Writer' was the UK number one on 23 June and US number one on 25 June.

There was a short German tour from 24 to 26 June 1966. German television station ZDF filmed one of the concerts

at the Circus Krone-Bau in Munich on 24 June. The programme, titled *Die Beatles*, was transmitted on 17 July, the set being 'Rock and Roll Music', 'Baby's in Black', 'I Feel Fine', 'Yesterday', 'Nowhere Man' and 'I'm Down'. The subsequent Japanese tour (27 June to 2 July) involved the group giving five concerts in Tokyo's Nippon Budokan Hall. Nippon Television filmed two shows, one on 30 June when the band were wearing dark suits (the 'black suits' show) and one on 1 July when the band were wearing light suits (the 'white suits' show'). Both concerts had identical playlists: 'Rock and Roll Music', 'She's a Woman', 'If I Needed Someone', 'Day Tripper', 'I Wanna Be Your Man', 'Baby's in Black', 'I Feel Fine', 'Yesterday', 'Nowhere Man', and 'I'm Down'. The Japanese tour was followed by the infamous visit to the Philippines, when the Beatles unknowingly offended the all-powerful Imelda Marcos, and were run out of town. A few moments of this disastrous trip were captured on silent newsreel footage.

The Beatles' last ever tour took place in North America from 12 to 31 August 1966. With their concert at San Francisco's Candlestick Park Stadium the group ceased touring. The songs 'Eleanor Rigby' and 'Yellow Submarine' were number one in the UK on 18 August.

In January 1967 the studio sessions for 'A Day in the Life' were filmed on 19 and 20 of the month and were later used for promos. At the end of the month (30 and 31 January) the Beatles worked on a promo film for 'Strawberry Fields Forever' at Knole Park in Kent. On 5 and 7 February they filmed a promo for 'Penny Lane' in Angel Lane, Stratford in the East End of London. Both short films, made by Swedish director Peter Goldmann, had a storyline and, in many people's opinion, were the first 'pop videos' – so familiar on MTV today. (The films directed by Michael Lindsay-Hogg for 'Rain' and 'Paperback Writer' may have a prior claim). A further promo was shot at London's Saville Theatre on 10 November, when the group, dressed in their Sgt. Pepper uniforms, played 'Hello, Goodbye'.

Opposite:
Rehearsing for *Thank Your Lucky Stars*,
28 March 1965

Above and opposite:
Rehearsals for *Thank Your Lucky Stars*,
28 March 1965

Opposite:
Rehearsing for *Blackpool Big Night Out*, 1 August 1965.
The puppet character at the front of the stage is Tivvy,
the popular mascot of *TV Times* magazine.

Above:
Rehearsing 'I'm Down' for *Blackpool Big Night Out*,
1 August 1965

Above and opposite:
The concert at the Circus Krone-Bau, Munich, 24 June 1966,
filmed by ZDF and transmitted as *Die Beatles* on 17 July

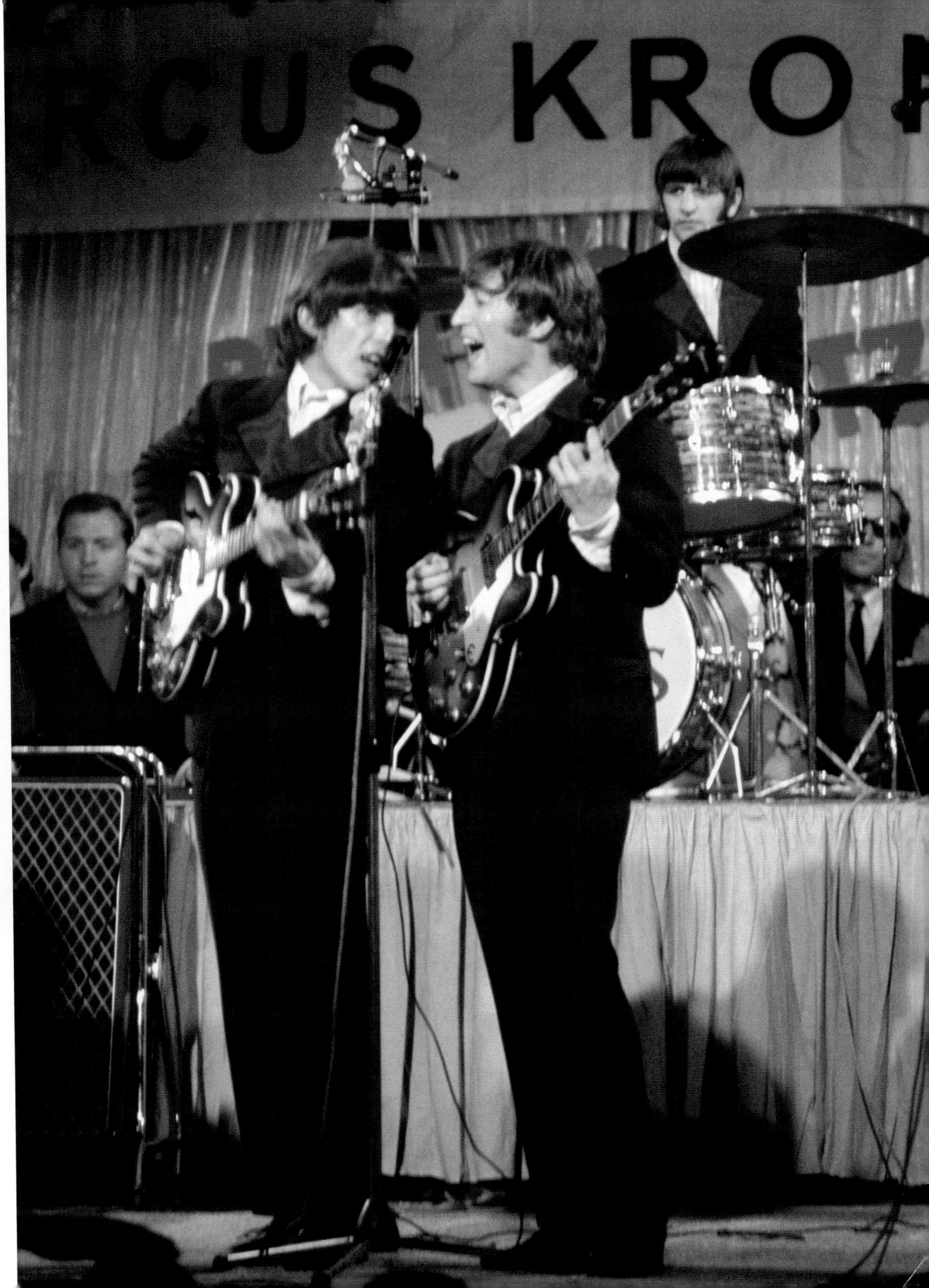
RCUS KRO

John as Dan the doorman, commissionaire of the Ad Lav club, 'London's most fashionable lavatory spot', in his second appearance on Peter Cook and Dudley Moore's *Not Only ... But Also*. Filmed in Berwick Street, London, on 27 November 1966, the sketch was transmitted on 26 December 1966.

George and John discuss Transcendental Meditation
with David Frost on *The Frost Programme*, 4 October 1967

1967: Our World

Our World, broadcast on 25 June 1967, was the first live international satellite television programme. Originally conceived by a BBC producer, Aubrey Singer, the project was transferred to the European Broadcasting Union. Ten months in the planning, a programme dedicated to international co-operation was dogged by the all-too-real international tensions of the period. One week before the broadcast the Eastern Bloc countries, led by the Soviet Union, pulled out as a protest against the Western nations' response to the Six Day War in the Middle East. In the end, 14 countries participated and the programme was beamed into 31 countries, using three satellites reaching an estimated audience of 400 million.

The ground rules specified that no politicians or heads of state could participate – and that everything had to be 'live'. The BBC had commissioned the Beatles to write a song for the UK's contribution. Both Paul and John wrote a lyric and then decided that John's was the most suitable. 'All You Need Is Love' had very simple lyrics (as specified by the BBC) and captured the mood of 1967's 'Summer of Love'. John Lennon was very interested in the power of slogans and the repetitiveness of the song shows how effective such a simple line can be. Asked in 1971 whether 'Give Peace a Chance' and 'Power to the People' were propaganda songs, John replied, 'Sure, so was 'All You Need Is Love'. I'm a revolutionary artist. My art is dedicated to change.'

The preparation for the broadcast of the finished song was complex. On 14 June the basic rhythm tracks and some vocal lines were laid down at Olympic Studios in London. The Beatles moved to EMI's Abbey Road studios on Monday 19 June to overdub lead and backing vocals, drums, piano and banjo. The orchestra began work on overdubs on Friday 23 June, in Studio Three. With the day of the broadcast fast approaching, Studio One was thrown open to the press on the morning of 24 June. In the afternoon there was a BBC camera rehearsal and later in the day further overdubs were made, following a decision to release 'All You Need Is Love' as a single.

Our World was transmitted in the UK from 7.55 to 10.00pm GMT, opening with the *Our World* theme sung in 22 languages by the Vienna Boys Choir. The first segment was from Canada – an interview with media guru Marshall McLuhan in a Toronto TV control room. Other segments included a Canadian rancher on his horse working his herd of cattle, the construction of the Tokyo underground, and the Australian Parkes Observatory tracking a deep space object.

The Beatles sequence started at 9.36pm. After an introduction, the cameras cut to the recording studio control room where George Martin asked the orchestra to come in. Once the musicians had filed in and settled down it was time for the all-important live performance, supported by the pre-recorded rhythm track.

With John, Paul and George perched on high stools and Ringo at his drum kit, Beatles and orchestra launched into 'All You Need Is Love'. The group were surrounded by friends seated on the floor creating a party atmosphere. Among the crowd were Mick Jagger, Marianne Faithful, Keith Richards, Keith Moon, Eric Clapton, Pattie Boyd, Jane Asher and Beatles biographer Hunter Davies. Streamers, balloons and banners added to the festive feel with much singing along and a final conga line.

'All You Need Is Love' was released as a single on 7 July in the UK and topped the chart on 19 July. It hit the number one spot in the US on 19 August. Much of the rest of 1967 was taken up with the production of the Beatles' *Magical Mystery Tour* project.

The *Our World* press call, Abbey Road Studios,
24 June 1967

John and Paul with Brian Epstein

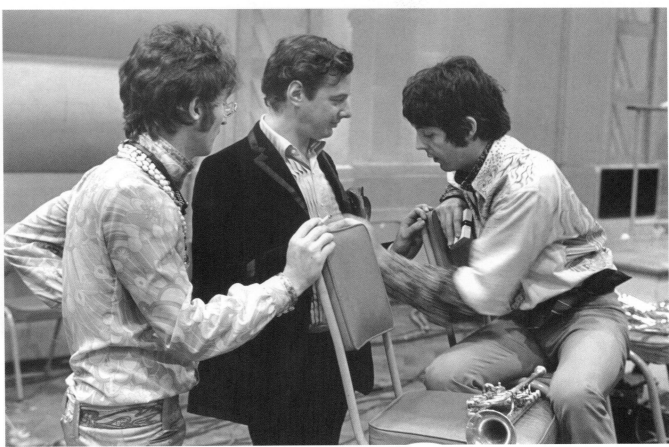

Brian Epstein (centre) and assistant Tony Bramwell (right)

Brian Epstein (left), producer George Martin
and recording engineer Geoff Emerick (right)

Epstein with Keith Moon and his wife, model Kim Kerrigan

Brian Epstein with George and his wife, model Pattie Boyd

Paul with girlfriend Jane Asher

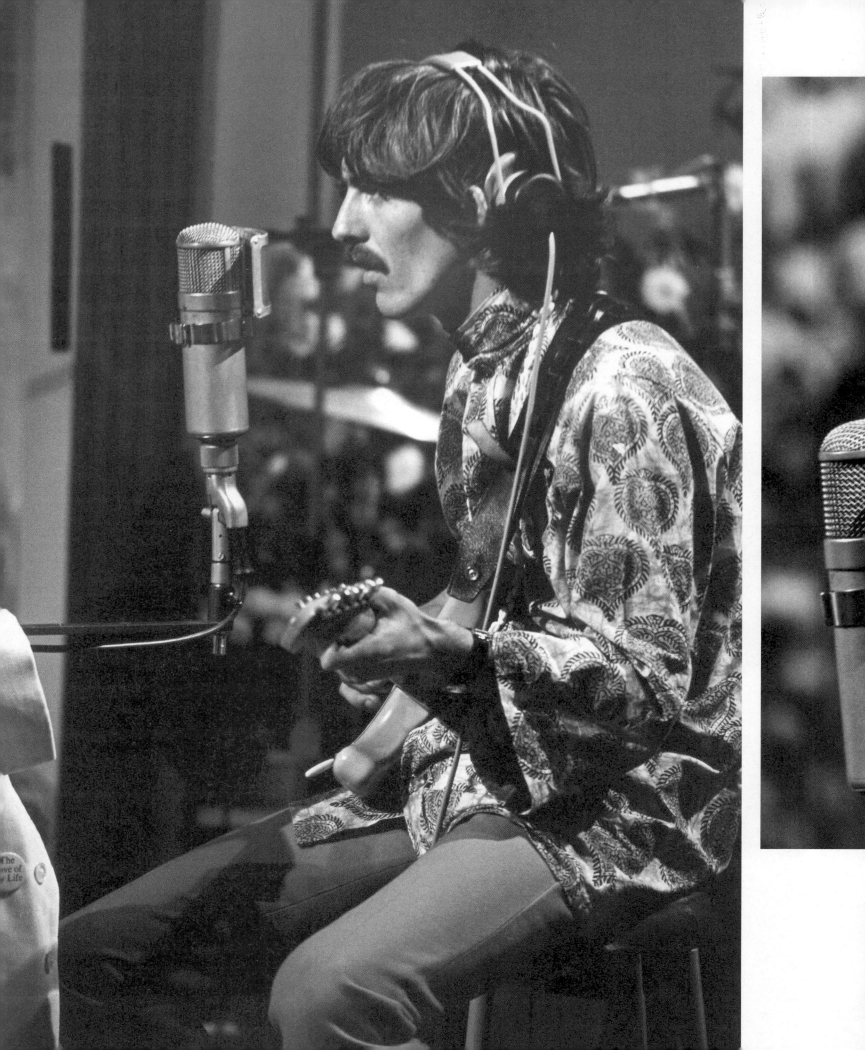

Paul celebrates the event's success with Jane Asher

John with Mick Jagger

1967:
Magical Mystery Tour

'I am concerned for you to enjoy yourselves,
within the limits of British decency.
You know what I mean, don't you?'

Buster Bloodvessel, aka Ivor Cutler,
addresses the passengers in *Magical Mystery Tour*

The Trip of a Lifetime

Magical Mystery Tour was originally conceived by Paul McCartney as a way of setting the Beatles a new challenge, a project that would carry them beyond the towering summit of *Sgt. Pepper*, into new creative territory.

Visiting California in April 1967, McCartney was intrigued by author Ken Kesey's travelling art troup The Merry Pranksters and their Dayglo touring coach 'Further' (The Merry Pranksters were themselves the subject of Tom Wolfe's book *The Electric Kool-Aid Acid Test*). In search of a new vehicle for the Beatles (literally), the shape of the movie was sketched out by McCartney on the plane journey back to England. The first song for the movie, 'Magical Mystery Tour', was begun on 25 April 1967, a mere four days after the Beatles had finished putting the final touches to *Sgt. Pepper*. This level of activity, however, was not sustained through the late spring and summer of 1967, the Beatles having other things on their minds. These included an unsuccessful trip to Greece in search of a private island hideaway, and the live global transmission of 'All You Need is Love' on 25 June – not to mention the general excitement of 1967's famous 'Summer of Love'. It was not until September – after the Beatles' first encounter with Transcendental Meditation and the sudden death of Brian Epstein – that work on the project gained serious momentum.

By this time, a cusp had been reached in the career of the Beatles, as well as in the buoyant and optimistic mood of Sixties Britain – which the Beatles themselves had done so much to focus and reflect. Britain was still hip, London still swung like nowhere else, but the first signs of a sea-change in the national mood were beginning to be visible. In July 1967, Rolling Stones Mick Jagger and Keith Richards were arrested and imprisoned for minor drug offences. The convictions were overturned, partly as a consequence of William Rees-Mogg's memorable lead article in the *Times*, which asked 'Who Breaks a Butterfly Upon a Wheel?' The zeitgeist of late 1967 could not be better illustrated than by what occurred next. On release from jail, the young television producer John Birt (later to be a controversial Director General of the BBC) arranged for Jagger to be flown by helicopter to a country house to attend a 'youth versus age' summit with representatives of the establishment which included Rees-Mogg himself, and the Bishop of Woolwich. The idea, difficult to understand for anyone who did not live through the social changes of the 1960s, was an attempt to orchestrate a debate on social values between concerned but tolerant defenders of the status quo, and the challenge to social order that Jagger was deemed to represent. But Jagger's libertarian position rather undercut the possibilities of cross-generational exchange:

JAGGER
(hesitant, with almost effeminate articulation)
...just in the very way I started myself,
when I was quite young...

REES-MOGG
(avuncular, encouraging tones)
Yes?

JAGGER
(continues more forcefully)
...which was to try and have as good a time as possible, which most young people do try and do, without regard for responsibilities of any sort...

The Bishop of Woolwich interjects a question which tries to draw Jagger into taking up some kind of social or political stance:

BISHOP
(adopting an expostulatory tone)
Do you think society today is more corrupt than it was, or do you think society has always been liable to be corrupt, and it is our duty to rebel against it?

JAGGER
(hesitant, non-committal)
Yes. I think it has always been corrupt.

Meanwhile, down in Weybridge, deep in Surrey's stockbroker belt, John Lennon had been improvising on his way towards a new song, but was rudely interrupted by the sound of a passing two-tone police siren. Incorporated into the composition, the siren mutated into the chord sequence of 'I Am the Walrus', the first of Lennon's songs to place the possession of enhanced or heightened awareness in fundamental opposition to an instinctively repressive establishment. 'I Am the Walrus', with its nagging riff and its sour synaesthesia, is the other side of the coin to the cheerful but lightweight 'Magical Mystery Tour'. 'Magical Mystery Tour' typifies McCartney's inclusive attitude. The Tour is presented as an excursion open to all: young and old, left and right, classless, regionless, with the tired and soon to be obsolescent holiday rituals of the Northern working class (they would soon discover Spain) redeemed and made magical through a burst of psychedelic music and sunshine. Lennon saw things differently. His most characteristic contribution to *Sgt. Pepper*, the verse and chorus progression of 'A Day in the Life', can be read as a lament that the mass of humanity blunder through their lives with their doors of perception permanently streaked with grime. For Lennon, isolated transcendent moments do not possess the power to change the world. Lennon consciously identifies and positions himself within a long tradition of isolated mystics whose visions are rejected by the mainstream and who are forced to pursue their destiny as the opposition party of the spirit. The public rejection of his dreams is what radicalizes the visionary – this seems to be the main theme of 'I Am the Walrus', and is a prophetic anticipation of the subsequent development of Lennon's career.

This tension, between the artist who sees it as their mission to heal social divisions, and the artist who accepts the role of caustic critic of society's squalid complacency – runs through *Magical Mystery Tour* like the letters through a stick of Blackpool rock. Rather than the surreal narrative and anti-naturalist editing (which British TV audiences could already enjoy every Saturday on *The Monkees* TV series), it is this Janus-faced attitude to its audience that is the most deeply disturbing aspect of the film. The audience is not given any clear signal of how it is expected to react to the spectacle it sees. *Magical Mystery Tour*, however unprofessional some of its direction and camera work may be, is a postmodernist work that forces the viewer to interpret and construct a narrative and a point of view from its kaleidoscope of disparate ingredients. Small wonder, then, that it proved to be so unpalatable for a BBC1 Boxing Day audience expecting some light entertainment from the Fab Four.

Opposite:
Paul with locals at Moorlands Garage & Café, Dartmoor, 12 September 1967

Above:
Ringo and Ivor Cutler

Opposite:
12 September – traffic gets snarled up on Dartmoor
as the Magical Mystery Tour takes a short cut that
goes horrible wrong when the bus is unable to
negotiate a narrow bridge

Ivor and Ringo take it easy on Dartmoor

Photographs taken on the Mystery Tour do seem to support the notion that Paul was the film's director

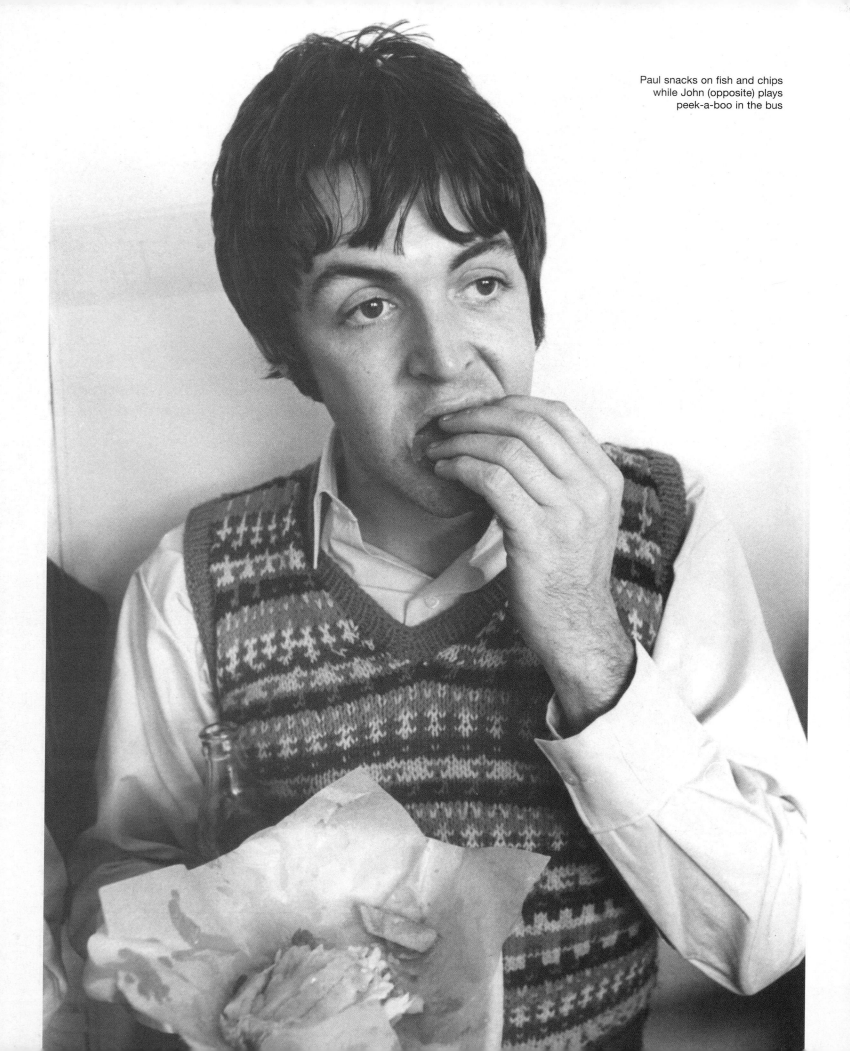

Paul snacks on fish and chips
while John (opposite) plays
peek-a-boo in the bus

Leaving the Atlantic Hotel, Newquay

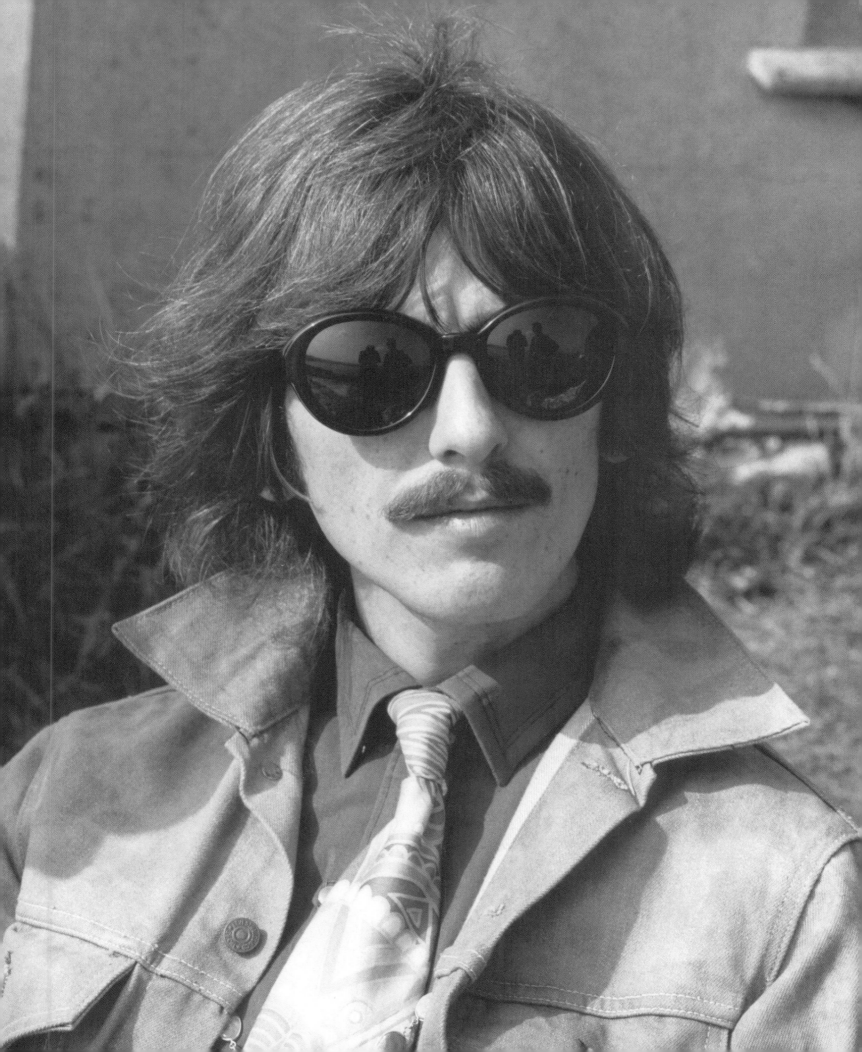

Above and opposite:
Filming in Newquay

Opposite:
Watergate Bay, 13 September – filming
the unused telescope sequence.
John discusses a set-up with
Production Manager Gavrik Losey.

Where's the Bus?

When intensive work finally began on *Magical Mystery Tour* in September 1967, the Beatles' circumstances were very changed. While studying Transcendental Meditation with the Maharishi in Bangor over the August Bank Holiday weekend, they had learned on 27 August of the sudden death of Brian Epstein. Cutting short their stay in Wales and hurrying back to London, the Beatles convened at McCartney's home in St John's Wood to consider a future without the manager who had taken care of their business interests since 1961. Among the many issues discussed at the meeting, a decision was reached, apparently steered through by McCartney, that the *Magical Mystery Tour* project should be given the full steam ahead, ready for a Christmas broadcast and record release. In what is described as an atmosphere of confusion bordering on panic, arrangements were made for the bus to go on the road and filming to begin on 11 September.

The actual Ken Kesey-style mystery tour with a real bus travelling through Devon and Cornwall was a relatively brief affair, lasting only from 11 to 15 September. The Beatles and their entourage spent only four nights away from London. Three of these were at the Atlantic Hotel in Newquay, which the band used as an impromptu base for most of their West Country filming. A relatively small proportion of the movie was actually shot out on the road, the key sequences filmed on location being the beach scene with Ivor Cutler and Jessie Robins, the magic tent scene (exterior, where the crowd files into the tent), and the beach scene with McCartney and George Claydon, which is intercut in the finished movie with the accordian singalong (actually filmed on the way back to London). Back in the home counties, the Beatles progressed to recording the remainder of *Magical Mystery Tour*'s songs, including a re-make of 'Your Mother Should Know', 'I Am the Walrus', 'Blue Jay Way', 'Flying' and 'The Fool on the Hill', as well as their next single 'Hello Goodbye', a

fragment of which also appears over the closing credits of *Magical Mystery Tour*.

There were also further scenes to shoot for the film itself. On 18 September, the Beatles joined the Bonzo Dog Doo-Dah band and stripper Jan Carson for the night club scenes, filmed in Soho's Raymond Revuebar. Thwarted in their attempt to book space at Shepperton Studios at short notice, the production went on location a second time from 19 to 24 September at West Malling Air Station. The ambience of this wartime airfield, with its imposing concrete anti-blast walls, and aircraft hangars commandeered as studio space, lends a distinctive appearance to some of the scenes filmed there. These included the 'Marathon' race sequence, the Magicians' laboratory, Aunt Jessie's spaghetti scene, George's cross-legged performance of 'Blue Jay Way', the superb exterior footage shot to accompany 'I Am the Walrus', and the big dance routine for 'Your Mother Should Know' which closes out the movie.

Work in the cutting rooms began on 25 September, with Roy Benson appointed as editor, with Mark Davis as his assistant, and with John and Paul taking a particularly close interest in post-production. There were also further scenes still to be shot, notably the introductory sequence with Ringo and Aunt Jessie (shot in Battersea on 29 October), Paul's mountain-top gyrations in the South of France to accompany 'The Fool on the Hill' (shot on 30 to 31 October) and the white cello scene from 'I Am the Walrus' and other shots for 'Blue Jay Way', filmed in Ringo's back garden on 3 November. Editing together this mass of disparate material, shot without the conventional regard for continuity, was a challenging task. Paul and John reputedly held opposing views about how scenes should be cut together. Nevertheless, the chaotic image that has attached itself so firmly to everything to do with *Magical Mystery Tour* is not wholly appropriate – 11 weeks for a fifty-minute mini-feature is hardly the longest ever stretch in post-production hell. The film was duly edited, dubbed and delivered to the BBC for its Boxing Day premiere.

The Magic Begins to Work

What kind of a film is *Magical Mystery Tour?* Why did it cause such confusion and offence when it was first screened?

The most regularly-repeated complaint from the *MMT* refuseniks was the lack of any discernable plot. This is a fair comment. The only strand in the film that resembles a traditional plotline is the romance between Aunt Jessie (Jessie Robins) and Buster Bloodvessel (Ivor Cutler), and this middle-aged love story was deemed by the BBC to be too unwholesome for family viewing, and thus was cut from the original screening. This lost plotlet aside, the film is structured around a series of brief vignettes, hung loosely around the progress of the coach trip, but in fact comprising a broad satirical onslaught against most of the cherished values of what was in those days known as 'straight' society.

The targets lampooned are, perhaps, predictable. They include the military mentality (the Victor Spinetti scenes, which are echoed by Buster Bloodvessel's attempts to take over as a more authoritarian tour courier). The film also satirizes the rat race and its roots in class conflict: observe how the men in suits – including a churchman – all jump the start of the marathon, and how some competitors enjoy a very unfair advantage in vehicles. Other targets include greed and consumerism (Aunt Jessie's food dream), the smiling face of stern authority (Derek Royle's jovial uniformed tour guide, the many references and cameos of policemen and other uniformed figures), jingoism (lots of byplay with that symbol of Swinging Sixties Britain, the Union Flag) and sexual repression (Ringo's arguments with his aunt, Paul's fumbling attempts to chat up Maggie Wright and his subsequent passage into daydream, Buster Bloodvessel's strangled declaration of passion, the masturbatory audience reactions to the stripper scene).

Weighed in the balance with these satirical targets are contrasting moments of humanity, innocence and warmth. These include small touches such as John's conversation with the little girl, group moments such as the accordian singalong, and the cross-generational finale with the Beatles in tails and the massed ballroom dancers and crisscrossing cadets of the Women's Royal Air Force all shaking a leg to 'Your Mother Should Know', one of McCartney's most calculating but memorable trans-generational anthems.

All of the above themes are packed tighter and punch their weight more effectively in the sequences specifically produced to go with *Magical Mystery Tour*'s songs, especially the footage that accompanies 'I Am the Walrus'. This forms a kind of film-within-a-film that recapitulates most of the themes of the movie as a whole. In these sequences, the Beatles were developing and perfecting the technique of subjective montage, intuitive jump cuts and surreal imagery which they had devised with Michael Lindsay-Hogg for 1966's 'Paperback Writer' and 'Rain' and Peter Goldman for 1967's 'Penny Lane' and 'Strawberry Fields Forever' promo films. These astonishingly inventive little films anticipate almost all of the techniques of the rock video, yet – subservient as they are to the songs which they accompany – they failed to provoke the negative reactions stirred up by *Magical Mystery Tour*. It seems as if the big public will happily enjoy surrealism and films which favour imagery over narrative, providing they do not go on for too long. And so long as there is a pretext (a song) on which to hang the anti-narrative material. Or perhaps – to put it another way – the big public is quite capable of loving the so-called avante-garde when it doesn't recognise what it is getting. Hence the popularity of the atonal orchestra crescendoes in 'A Day in the Life' and the unpopularity of the sound collage 'Revolution 9', the Beatles' 1968 sonic counterpart to *Magical Mystery Tour*.

Paul's scene at Porth Beach, filmed on 13 September.
Eventually intercut with the singalong sequence on the bus.

The deleted Rubber Man scene, filmed by the pool at the Atlantic Hotel, Newquay, on 13 September

Warming up after a swim in the Atlantic Hotel's open air pool

Don't Get Historical on Me

Much has been made of the BBC's decision to screen *Magical Mystery Tour* on 26 December on BBC1, at a time when only their other channel, BBC2, was equipped for colour transmission. Some commentators go as far as to suggest that the BBC's decision effectively sabotaged *Magical Mystery Tour*'s impact, as the film needed to be seen in colour to be fully appreciated. This latter point is undoubtedly true, but to blame the BBC is to be completely unaware of the circumstances of British television in 1967. Although the first country in Europe to adopt colour television (BBC2 was the first channel to transmit in colour, beginning in June 1967), UK ownership of colour sets did not reach the 100,000 level until September 1968. Therefore, considerably less than one percent of the Beatles' 15 million viewers in December 1967 had the wherewithal to watch *Magical Mystery Tour* in colour. Furthermore, BBC2 was regarded by the television public as a minority channel, screening largely inaccessible, highbrow programmes. To bury a new Beatles film on BBC2, at a time when only a tiny percentage of viewers could benefit from its colour technology, would have been a senseless piece of holiday scheduling. By rapidly rescreening *Magical Mystery Tour* on 5 January, this time on BBC2 and in colour (allegedly after complaints from Ringo Starr!), the Beeb probably made the best of a bad job.

In the 1960s, colour movies were routinely screened in black and white on television, as well as being panned-and-scanned to fit television's aspect ratio. Nobody complained. It was an accepted limitation of the medium. Clearly, watching *Magical Mystery Tour* in black and white is a major diminution of the experience, but it is a perverse misreading of the evidence to suggest that this was the chief reason for the film's adverse critical reception in 1967. Something more fundamental in the content was rubbing people the wrong way.

And the World Said...

'Blatant rubbish.' *The Daily Express*
'Chaotic.' *The Daily Mirror*
'It's colossal, the conceit of the Beatles.' *The Daily Mail*

'I was absolutely furious after seeing the Beatles' *Magical Mystery Tour*. How anyone can pay out money – our money, the licence holders – for such rubbish is beyond me. I would not give 2d for it. It was too stupid for words.'

Mrs H Murray, Walthamstow, London, E17
Letter to *Disc & Music Echo*'s Pop Post

'I couldn't make sense of some of the *Magical Mystery Tour* but did it really need to make sense? ... Does everything have to make sense to be enjoyed? Party political broadcasts on TV are hard enough to understand and are not enjoyable.'

Miss B Toole, Liverpool Street, London
Letter to *Disc & Music Echo*'s Pop Post

'At last the Beatles have finally outsmarted the British public with the most fantastic and original TV show ever, proving once again they are the world's greatest performers.'

David Palmer, Billingham, Co.Durham
Letter to *Disc & Music Echo*'s Pop Post

'Couldn't those stupid people who complained about it see the beauty and sense of it? There were many messages to see in it and as for having no story – so what! The Beatles triumphed because they dared to show the human mind from the inside.'

Ray Dexter, Hoddesdon, Herts
Letter to *Disc & Music Echo*'s Pop Post

'The arrogance of the critics who contemptuously dismissed *Magical Mystery Tour* as the biggest load of rubbish ever seen on television amazes me. Certainly it was not the film masterpiece of 1967. But the opinions voiced only seem to reflect the all too [common] rejection of anything which does not conform to established ideals. Is it a crime to be an individual?'

Barry Moore, Beckingham, Kent
Letter to *Disc & Music Echo*'s Pop Post

'I am not a great Beatles fan but I thought it was one of the most professional and enjoyable TV programmes of the year. Are people so stupid as to need the plot printed in capital letters to be satisfied with the programme?'

Peter Taylor, Royton, Oldham, Lancs
Letter to *Disc & Music Echo*'s Pop Post

'The Beatles have made the biggest mistake of their careers. It was hopeless to think families sitting round the box on Boxing Day full of Christmas cheer would understand the intricate thought and construction behind it. "The Magical Mystery Tour is waiting to take you away" they said – but no one was waiting to go. It failed because no one seemed to understand the magic. Magic doesn't happen to you, it happens for you...'

A R Wooster, High Wycombe, Bucks
Letter to *Disc & Music Echo*'s Pop Post

Since their emergence into superstardom in 1963, the Beatles had enjoyed a charmed relationship with Britain's frequently vitriolic media. As a national institution that affirmed the country's creative vitality and progressive social attitudes, it seemed as if they could do no wrong – even when others in the upper echelons of the pop pantheon were being busted left, right and centre. Nevertheless, it is remarkable that the Beatles believed that the mass Boxing Day TV audience could readily digest something as outré as *Magical Mystery Tour* along with its cold turkey and re-heated Christmas pudding. Whatever their expectations for the film's reception, it is implausible to suggest that the Beatles no longer cared what the big public thought of their work, as the scathing reviews from the mainstream TV critics elicited what amounted to a public defence of the programme from McCartney on *The David Frost Show*. Unsurprisingly, the pop press and its readership were far more positive, many acclaiming the film as a triumph. As Ian McDonald astutely points out in *Revolution in the Head*, this opposing reaction from the mainstream media and the pop fan base signalled the end of the trans-generational consensus on the Beatles. The loveable moptops had suddenly become agents for the subversion of established order.

Left and opposite:
The excised George Harrison meditation scene, 14 September

Below:
Putting up the magic tent, 14 September.
The tent itself is clearly visible behind Ringo's legs.

Ringo warms up for the tent scene
with a bit of football practice.
Derek Royle and Mandy Weet
are to the right.

Acanthus Road, Battersea, 29 October 1967:
Ringo and his Aunt Jessie show up for the start of the Mystery Tour

Derek Royle, Mandy Weet and Ringo
help Aunt Jessie on to the tour bus

Sunny Heights (Ringo's residence), 3 November:
the white cello footage from the
'I Am the Walrus' sequence

1968-1970: The End

Much of the early part of 1968 was taken up with the Beatles' trip to India, and with the setting up of Apple, their idealistic multi-directional creative corporation and management umbrella.

By the middle of 1968, the Beatles were beginning to come apart. The death of Brian Epstein and the diverging interests of the Fab Four meant that the spirit of peace and harmony was sadly lacking. During the year, only three promo sessions were held. On 11 February the group were filmed in the studio recording 'Hey Bulldog', the material being used for 'Lady Madonna' and 'Hey Bulldog' promos. An Apple Records promo film recorded Paul running through 'Blackbird' and part of 'Helter Skelter' on 13 June 1968. Finally, on 4 September, the group were at Twickenham Studios recording live performance promos for 'Hey Jude' (three versions) and 'Revolution' (2 versions).

By the beginning of 1969 relationships were so strained that Paul suggested the idea of producing a live or recorded eight-song one-hour television show in front of a live audience (the kind of event that had, in the past, stimulated the group). So it was that the Beatles assembled at Twickenham Film Studios on 2 January to start rehearsing new songs for the television show which had the working title *Get Back*. The rehearsals were filmed, directed by Michael Lindsay-Hogg, who had also been engaged to direct the concert film, for a planned documentary. The group spent much of the time from 2 to 15 January trying things out in the studio with no particular direction. The tensions between the members of the band were obvious, and can be seen on the released documentary. On 10 January George walked out and, after a meeting to clear the air, the project changed – the cameras would remain but they would, instead, film a new album being produced at Apple's studio and the whole thing would be turned into a feature film. *Let It Be* (as the film was re-titled) finally consisted of a series of sequences including some of the Twickenham footage, three songs recorded in the Apple basement studio, various non-musical clips of the Beatles and, finally, the famous rooftop concert, filmed on the roof of Apple's Savile Row headquarters. At the end of the set (and the end of the film) John stepped forward and said 'I'd just like to say "thank you" on behalf of the group and ourselves and I hope we have passed the audition.' At that point the frame freezes as a reprise of 'Get Back' plays over the closing titles.

Let It Be premiered on 20 May 1970 at the London Pavilion cinema. None of the Beatles attended. On 10 April 1970 it had become official – the group had split up.

Opposite:
The premiere of *Let It Be* at the London Pavilion, 20 May 1970

Above and opposite:
McCartney and Lennon are interviewed by guest host Joe Garagiola and
actress Tallulah Bankhead on NBC's *The Tonight Show starring Johnny
Carson*, 14 May 1968 – Carson was on holiday

'I think they're very serious fellows.'
Tallulah Bankhead to Joe Garagiola,
The Tonight Show, 14 May 1968

21 December 1967, Westbourne Suite, Royal Lancaster Hotel.
Ringo, John and Paul with Maureen Starkey (left) and Jane Asher (right) at
a fancy-dress party to celebrate the completion of *Magical Mystery Tour*.

Afterword

So close is the association between The Beatles and the 1960s, that it is often seen as inevitable – as well as opportune – that their career did not continue into the following decade. Yet other iconic artists of the sixties – Bob Dylan, The Rolling Stones – were able to produce work during the 1970s that is, arguably, the equal of their best output. If the Beatles had felt moved to stay together, there is no way to tell how they might have responded to the social climate of the new decade – no way to second guess how that very different era might have been reflected in their music.

But the Beatles did break up: effectively in 1969, formally in 1970. One result of this is that – with hindsight – their relatively brief career seems to be inextricably tied in with the social and cultural changes of the era which they did so much to shape, as well as to express. The journey from the 1963 Royal Command Performance to *Magical Mystery Tour* seems immense in terms of the social changes reflected – yet the two television events were only four years apart in time.

Television had grown up and changed around the Beatles. Major bands no longer deigned to appear on middle-of-the-road variety shows. The televising of pop groups had dropped such patronising formats as the convention of the fake interview – the phoney question-and-answer rituals usually orchestrated by an older, 'straight' presenter who spoke perfect Queen's English. By the late sixties, regional accents had become part of the norm on British television, a process which the Beatles had had some part in accelerating. And the suited, short-haired compère of the early sixties (think of Pete Murray in the early years of *Top of the Pops*, or even Keith Fordyce in *Ready, Steady, Go!*) had been replaced by DJs who were as long-haired and flamboyantly-dressed as the bands they introduced: Tony Blackburn, Jimmy Savile, John Peel. And, of course, colour television had arrived, with all of its possibilities for abstract graphics and MTV-style video footage. As often as not, the music was left to speak for itself.

And, arguably, there matters might have rested. That is, until another musical revolution arrived, one which again used television as its most potent PR tool. The Sex Pistols' notorious Bill Grundy interview took place a mere seven years after the Beatles split up. But it belongs to a totally different social climate, almost to a different cultural epoch. Yet – some might argue – the seeds of the Sex Pistols' all-out attack on the citadels of media power were sown through the changes forced onto British television by the advent of the Beatles. As they always say, you can't put the genie back inside the bottle.

Looking beyond the 1970s to more recent decades, the Beatles' greatest television legacy could be said to be the development of the pop video. As George Harrison remarks in *The Beatles Anthology*: 'We invented MTV'. Although – arguably – the Beatles might have overstretched the imagination of their audience with the *Magical Mystery Tour*, the incisive, kaleidoscopic imagery and editing of the 'Rain', 'Paperback Writer', 'Penny Lane' and 'Strawberry Fields Forever' videos are a timeless achievement that makes much of what has come after seem almost redundant.

The Beatles may have split up in 1970, but the Beatles cult was just getting into its stride. As Hunter Davies points out in his updated official biography, the Beatles now provide gainful employment for around one hundred times more persons than when they were together as a group. This Beatles cult, and its associated Beatles industry, shows no signs of disappearing as we near the end of the first decade of the 21st century.

At some (hopefully distant) point in the future, the uneven and sometimes unrepresentative film and TV footage of the Beatles will be the only way for a new generation to witness what the members of the band were like in person. Viewed as a whole, the collected TV material is a curious mish-mash: concise, intense, contradictory, unforgettable, and over much too soon. At least in that way, the TV legacy is a true reflection of the Beatles' overall career.

Further Reading and Other Resources

There are, of course, literally thousands of books about The Beatles – not to mention films, tv shows, fanzines and websites. This is not the place to list all of them. However, the standard works on The Beatles are fewer in number, and well worth exploring if you have not encountered them already. We have also included some works of particular relevance to The Beatles' television career.

Books

The Beatles, Hunter Davies, Norton, first edition 1968,
    fourth edition 1996
The Beatles Anthology, Cassel, 2000
The Beatles Film & TV Chronicle 1961-1970,
    Jörg Pieper and Volker Path, Premium Publishing, 2005
The Complete Beatles Chronicle, Mark Lewisohn,
    Chancellor Press, 1996
John Winston Lennon (1940-66) and *John Ono Lennon*
    (1966-80), Ray Coleman, Sidgwick and Jackson,
    two volumes, 1984
Lennon Remembers, Jann Wenner, Verso, 1972
Paul McCartney – Many Years From Now, Barry Miles,
    Secker and Warburg, 1997
Revolution in the Head, Ian MacDonald, Fourth Estate,
    first edition 1994
Those Were the Days: An Unofficial History of the Beatles'
    Apple Organization, Stefan Granados,
    Cherry Red Books, 2002
The Unknown Paul McCartney, Ian Peel, Reynolds & Hearn,
    2002

Films & TV Shows

These are The Beatles' official film and television releases. The complete *Anthology*, at a mighty 660 minutes, contains an enormous amount of essential Beatles material unavailable elsewhere.

The Beatles: A Hard Day's Night (1964)
The Beatles: Help! (1965)
The Beatles: Magical Mystery Tour (1967)
The Beatles: Yellow Submarine (1968)
The Beatles: Let It Be (1970)
The Beatles: Anthology (1995)

The Internet

The internet is bursting with Beatles-related material. These are a very small selection of those websites we have found useful.

www.beatles.com
www.johnlennon.com
www.paulmccartney.com
www.georgeharrison.com
www.ringostarr.com
    These are the official websites.

www.beatles.net
    A useful portal, with links to many Beatles resources.
www.beatlesstory.com
    The website of The Beatles Story museum in Liverpool, containing much else besides.
www.jpgr.co.uk/mmt.html
    The website of The Magical Mystery Tour, who organise Beatles-themed tours in and around Liverpool.
www.geocities.com/~beatleboy1
    The Beatles Ultimate Experience: an unofficial website containing a vast selection of material.
www.marmalade-skies.co.uk
    A website dealing with sixties British psychedelia in general, which contains much of both direct and indirect relevance to the latter part of The Beatles' career.

Picture Credits

All references are by page numbers.

Rex Features: front cover, 2, 4, 5, 6, 8-10, 12, 15, 16,
    18-38, 41-58, 61-72, 74-120, 123-135, 137-143,
    145-148, 150-168, 170-172, 175, back cover
Lillian Evans: 166 (top)
Mal Evans: 120, 162-165, 166 (bottom), 167
Everett Collection: 38, 44
Harry Goodwin: 45, 46 (top)
Reg Gould: 46 (bottom), 47
ITV: 8, 9, 26, 27, 30-37, 41-43, 71, 175
Keystone USA: 70, 130, 131, 172
David Magnus: front cover, 2, 16, 24, 25, 28, 29, 53, 54,
    72, 74-77, 78-119
David McEnery: 168
NBCU Photo Bank: 170, 171
Terry O'Neill: 12, back cover
Bill Orchard: 68, 69
David Redfern: 4, 61-63, 123-129, 132-135, 137, 143,
    145-148, 150-161
Peter G Reed: 64-67
Rex USA: 57
Richard Rosser: 6, 55, 56
Sipa Press: 23
Michael Ward: 10
Reg Wilson: 78

Clowning around with Eric Morecambe and Ernie Wise
during rehearsals for *The Morecambe and Wise Show*,
2 December 1963

Index